I0448728

MY
CONNECTIONS
MAGAZINE SUMMER 2014

myconnectionsmagazine.com online and Learn
more weconnect2.com   YOU ARE WHAT YOU WARE
Show time always

Publisher Eddie Elchahed. Free Classified Ads from
News U.S Journal nusjournal.com
and anaheimpublishing.CO Inside more details, and
special offers

Feature story
The making of "St Jude Children Research Hospital"
Top Hotel Destinations
Cheap Vegas Hotel From $23.00
Give the gift that save lives
donate to "Doctors Without Borders"
Helping over 70 countries during Civil wars, Natural and man made Disasters,
and the spread of deadly contiguous epidemics
Inside and more hot topics and special offers
My Connections Magazine is about Main Stream people and their experience with:
Diet Connections, Fashion Connections, Places Connections, and Social Trends Connections.

Introduction

My Connections Magazine is a publication on a quarterly basis unless otherwise special circumstances needed to bring you more or immediate coverage of upcoming events.

This publication cove the headlines in weconnect.com a learning website about almost everything that touch our social life on day to day basis. Overall Study on the needs to read in print beside the all out digital revolution of about everything, most people are concern to continue to share with old adults some of the current experiences, news, and different events.

Social media and digital publications all on any devices and desktops gadgets are somehow not yet entirely accepted by the old adults population. Most companies are expecting a five years

minimum turnaround for the full digital revolution to take charge of all of us including all that

of old adults population.

We therefore focus more on the issues that continue to have total effect on all of us regardless what means of communications is used to channel our information that we share with everyone. Diet is our most talked subject among all those we connect with everywhere and of all ages. Diet is about food, losing hat fat, looking our best, and all that to evolve around diet from exercise, to nutrition supplements, and fun or rest as a necessary element of anything beside diet.

Yes, fashion statement is of an equal important because as we all know by now, that we are what we ware. The statement can make or break one skill to communicate among others, from family members, friends, and coworkers. If your day was to depend on your uniform, make it that of a habit on everyday as you depend equally on your casual clothing too.

Places and social trends are both a common destination everyone talk about, dream about, and share the experience with others to influence those who really want to be part of your personal life. For example, what would like Disneyland, if you are the only one who knew about it. Monday usually the talk about places and social trends, as the weekend set for the adventure to explore others favorite places, and to learn or be part of a social trend such as a combination of what the place is about.

Well, to share with you my experience of a social trend and relevant or irrelevant to the placei visit, is South Coast Plaza. People who you see around anywhere at or in the vicinity of SCP have things in common socially than other people elsewhere. Dining, Clothing, cars, and socializing are those you can see from close distance, keeping in mind the living style or residential status they all press about for a more affluent address as a show down among them.

We hope to entertain you and bring the best to you in every publication and in every issue we put out in print or digital. Our best, make it simple and fresh online website to better serve you. What would you say of all the years we used and abused our planet, waiting for today online simple and fresh web and internet? we hope that we are there too for our readers, online visitors, subscribers, and customers. That we are as concern as everyone else.

Table of Content

Eddie Adel
Chief Executive Officer
My Connections Magazine
Email:
weconnect2@live.com

How to Become Taller Naturally

Maybe you feel like your friends have suddenly hit a growth spurt and you're lagging seriously behind. Maybe the rest of your family is really tall and you're wondering if you can do anything to catch up. The truth is that a person's height is mostly determined by things out of their control,-- genes.

Do know, though, that there are many factors that affect height *which can be controlled*, a whole battery of natural habits, techniques and foods that can enhance your ability to grow taller. So, if you are still growing, read on to learn about natural ways that work for and with you to help you grow taller.

What are growth spurts?

Growth spurts is a term used for a rapid increase in height and weight which typically occurs during puberty.In their teens, kids put on an amazing growth to reach their final adult height. This phenomenal growth starts at the outside of the body and works in. Hands and feet are the first to expand. Needing new shoes is the first sign of experiencing growth spurts. Next, arms and legs grow longer. Finally the spine grows. The very last expansion is a broadening of the chest and shoulders in boys, and a widening of the hips and pelvis in girls.

What kind of a diet can help increase my height?

A nutritious diet that includes fruits and vegetables, dairy, cereals, meat, and plenty of water will aid the natural process for enhancing height.

. **Does sleep help human growth?**

Getting proper sleep is vital for the growth hormones to perform its function effectively. Not getting enough sleep can lower the amount of growth hormones your body produces.

. **What are growth hormones?**

Human growth hormone (HGH) is a substance released by a pea like structure deep inside the brain just behind the eyes. This substance is mostly released during the first couple of hours of sleep and after exercise. Its function is to stimulate growth in human body up until the end of puberty.

. **Can the intake of growth hormones (HGH) make me grow taller?**

The intake of growth hormones can work only during the formative years. The excessive intake of hormones through artificial means may cause abnormal and disproportionate growth. The term (HGH) has often been used and abused by many fraudulent marketers to make outrageous claims of stimulating growth. The fact is that the sale of growth hormone treatment is highly regulated and can only be prescribed by specialists.

. **Are there any medications that can help me gain height after puberty?**

There is no medication that can make you enhance height after puberty. There are many products in the market today that claim to increase height of adults, but they are all scams without sufficient scientific evidence.

. **Can stretching exercises help me gain height?**

Some stretching exercises can help increase the height enhancing process during puberty. After puberty the stretching exercises can still help correct a person·s posture. You·ll be surprised by how much of *Height* is hidden behind your slouched back. You can, at any age, add an inch or two of height by simply improving your posture. Follow the link below for information on specific height enhancing exercises:

Heare some final questions and answers to grow taller ...

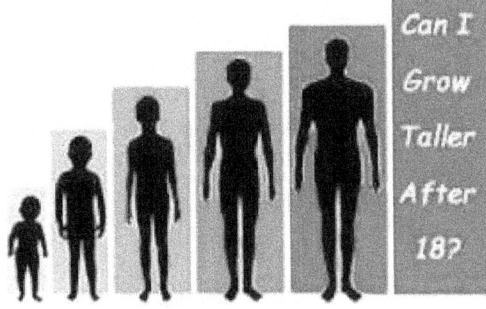

Is it true that the present generation is taller than the previous one?

There seems to be a correlation between *economic growth* and *human height*. Asian populations were once thought to be inherently shorter; though it now seems that the average height of China and other Asian countries have improved significantly. The human growth responds to better health care facilities and better nutritional diet. The following chart will help you understand the increase in average human height during the last 150 years:

	1850	2000
USA (White)	5'.8"	5'.10"
USA (Black)	5'.6"	5'.9"
Canada	5'.7"	5'.10"
Sweden	5'.6"	5'.11'

Germany	5'.6"	5'.10"
England	5'.5"	5'.9"
Denmark	5'.5"	6'.0"
Czech	5'.5"	5'.11"
Netherlands	5'.5"	6'.0"
France	5'.4"	5'.9"

. What should be my ideal weight with regards to my height?

According to the rule of the thumb the <u>ideal weight of Men</u> can be calculated as under:

For the first 5 feet the weight should be 106 pounds. And for each additional inch add 6 pounds.

The <u>ideal weight of Women</u> can be calculated as under:

For the first 5 feet the weight should be 100 pounds. And for each additional inch add 5 pounds.

. Does body building stunt human growth?

There is no scientific evidence available to prove that weight training may stunt human growth. There are people like *Shaquille O'Neal, David Robinson, Arnold Schwarzenegger,* and many more who started bodybuilding at an early age and yet still were able to attain an above average height.

. How to find the height of my favorite celebrity?

You can visit the link below to find the height of many celebrities:

. Fashion ideas that can make me look taller?

Looking Taller and Slimmer is an art that can be mastered by following a few simple fashion guidelines. The following quiz has been designed to help kick start your fashion sense. Answer the *True & False* questions for a guided tour of how to dress for a taller look:

. What is Heightism?

Heightism is a type of discrimination based on human height. This refers to unfair treatment because of a person's short or tall stature. Short people are generally disadvantaged for employment opportunities. For most women, the height of a man is a major factor that makes him sexually attractive towards her. Heightism is also cited as one of the underlying causes of the Rwandan Genocide, in which approximately one million people were killed. It is believed that one of the reasons that political power was conferred to the minority Tutsis by the exiting Belgians was because they were taller and therefore (in the eyes of the Belgians) considered superior and more suited to governance. Short candidates face disadvantage in politics too. Out of the 54 US presidential elections only 13 have been won by the shorter candidate.

. **Do astronauts get taller in space?**

Since there is no (or little) gravity in space the bones of the astronauts are less squashed together. The astronauts, therefore, do gain a bit of height due to this fact.

MY DIET CONNECTIONS
Best way to burn fat----

Best Ways To Burn Fat

The best ways to burn fat will be different for each unique individual, as we all have different metabolisms, and different physical characteristics. Nevertheless, there are some common principles which can be applied to anyone, and it these that we shall concentrate on here. The methods given here are tested over time, and among the best ways to burn fat.

Method 1

The most obvious form of exercise you can perform is still one of the best ways to burn fat, and that is simple running. This running can be done indoors on a treadmill, but you will probably burn more calories by getting outside. If you do your running in the countryside, across country and often on hilly terrain, you will be working your body hard, and in a healthy environment.

Method 2

There is no doubt that skipping is one of the best ways to burn fat, if not the best. Successive generations of boxers have incorporated skipping into their daily schedule, and these are people who can afford to be at anything below peak fitness. If you practice skipping for twenty minutes, you will probably find it the hardest 20 minutes of your training career!

Method 3

One of the best ways to burn fat is to know what you are setting out to do All physical exercise takes effort and determination, and you are far more likely to succeed if you can know what you have to do to reach your target. On average you need to burn 3500 calories to lose a pound of fat. There is also a formula which says if you multiply your weight in pounds by 13, you will find out the number of calories it will take for you to stay at your current weight. If you play around with the numbers a little, you can get an idea of how many calories you need to be taking in each day to lose the fat you want to lose. From these formulae, you can work out a reasonable plan for burning fat and losing weight.

Method 4

The best ways to burn fat will always be ways you are likely to stick with, so if you are keen on intense sport, take advantage of this. Even if you only perform the activity in short bursts, you will still be burning calories. There is a lot of running and exertion involved in virtually any sport, and most have practice drills which you can perform alone. Doing something which gives you a challenge, and which you find satisfying, will give you the drive to push through the bad times and carry on.

These four methods are the best ways to burn fat.

Everything about losing weight begin in the kitchen. Now enjoy a digital copy of "Belly Flat Six Pack 7, 8" for only $2.99 available at nusjournal .com When you browse our News U.S. Journal at nusjournal.com you find new products also in the digital store online.

Five Great Exercise Machines for Burning Fat

These exercise machines are related to cardiovascular and aerobic workouts. The equipment listed here allows for more challenges and more variety in your exercise routines. These machines are great for anyone looking to lose weight and improve their overall health.

Some advanced exercising machines include electronic devices that measure your weight before and after you do the exercise, the amount of calories you burned, time elapsed, heart rate, and other useful information. Let's look at what these mackines are and what benefits they provide. Treadmill:

A treadmill is an exercising device consisting of an endless belt on which a person can walk or jog with or without changing pace . It is supported by a sturdy deck propelled either by an electric motor or by the user. It generally has some shock absorption system, usually rubber cushioning, to minimize stress on your joints.

Using a treadmill will speed up your metabolic rate and allow your body to absorb and utilize greater quantities of the nutrients that you consume. It will also help to stabilize your blood pressure and blood sugar as well as increase your energy level.
When using a treadmill to burn fat and lose weight, you need to exercise on a daily basis.

A treadmill helps you burn more calories by increasing your exercise frequency. It gives you a LOT of workout versatility. You can start with a slow walk and then speed it up as your body gets into better shape, and there are also various incline levels to provide extra resistance when you become more advanced. By using the large muscles of the legs, a treadmill helps you burn more fat calories.

Elliptical Trainer:

Elliptical trainers are exercise machines which combine the natural stride of a treadmill and the simplicity of a stair climber. On an Elliptical trainer, you stand comfortably in an upright position while holding onto the machine's handrails and striding in either a forward or reverse motion.

The elliptical trainer burns more calories than either the treadmill or the exercise bike. With an elliptical cross trainer, you get the benefits of both aerobic and resistance exercises without the wear and tear on your joints. It provides a great cardio workout that pumps you heart to the max without the strain and stress on your joints. It uses all of the muscles of the lower leg. Therefore, you will strengthen and build your lower legs. This is an ideal workout for those exercisers out there who are overweight and do not want to jog.

Exercise Bikes:

There are two types of exercise bikes you can use, upright bikes and recumbent bikes. Upright bikes simulate the action of a real bike except you do not go anywhere. Recumbent bikes on the other hand, have bucket seats which have the pedals out in front of you. Exercise bikes are great for cardiovascular fitness and toning or building your thighs. The recumbent bikes are especially good for toning your butt. Being stationary, you can enjoy your favorite magazine or TV program while working out.

For overweight people, the recumbent bike offers bucket seats which can be more comfortable than traditional uprights. This type of bike is more ergonomically correct than a traditional upright exercise bike and an effective way to improve aerobic capacity, as well as burn fat. Plus, it offers more back support and may be a little more comfortable to those people with lower back pain.

Rowers:

There are two types of rowing machines. A hydraulic machine uses a piston to provide the resistance. With a cable-driven machine, your pull spins a flywheel which produces a smooth action similar to rowing on water. The smoothness of the flywheel creates little strain on the back. If handles are not adjusted properly for height differences, hydraulic rowers can create back strain.

Rowing machines provide a whole-body aerobic workout: arms, shoulders, back, abdomen, legs, heart and lungs. It also builds muscle strength and endurance in addition to the aerobic benefits.

It improves your whole cardiovascular system with a low impact workout. Other benefits include improved flexibility and muscle strengthening in the arms, abdomen, and back.

Steppers:

Steppers are available as simple hydraulic steppers or as computerized stair steppers. It tones the buttocks, thighs and hips. These are the areas that, paticularly in women, have a tendency to "balloon" from too many calories and not enough exercise. Stair stepper workouts are calorie burners that rank as one of the best cardiovascular exercises for people of all ages and fitness levels.

We expanded to suit your need. Come on in for a visit. we ae in the City of Garden Grove CA, on Chapman Ave, and West St, next to Certified Market..Inside Studio B.

3 Simple Steps To Lose Body Fat

What Does It Take To Lose Body Fat?

To lose body fat, you need to incorporate sheer simplicity, plus ultimate science because understanding how to lose body fat comprises your awareness of BOTH concepts. Now is the time to prepare your heart and mind for non-stop challenge, consistent focus, and utmost care.

You are here seeking some viable remedy, correct? Our time together here is far more worthwhile if I just go ahead and tell you, right now, what it takes to lose body fat. In a nutshell, your biggest key is mental preparedness. Yep. That's the biggie!

As soon as you discover how to convince your mind to issue "lose body fat" commands, you are well on your way to fitness success. To lose body fat, then, is a quite simple matter. Ye, of course, the difficulty you may face lies in your initial THINKING, then the reality of DOING.

There are a few things you will have to do in order to lose body fat. If and when you are willing and ready to do these things, you are SURE to lose body fat, without question.

LONG-TERM "LOSE BODY FAT" SOLUTION

Does It Really Pay To Seek A Short Cut To Lose-Body-Fat Satisfaction?

After you spin yourself virtually all the way around in a lose-body-fat circle by asking questions from sources that either really don't know the truth, or even worse, only care to tell whatever it takes to separate you from your checkbook, credit card, or wallet -- the simplicity and long-time duality of how to lose body fat remains unchanged. Ease versus complexity... long way around versus short-cut solution.

Somebody or someone (meaning YOU) has to do the work! You want to lose body fat, that's why you're here. So, your body needs to engage required, time proven, professional principles that prove themselves for you over and again. In short, to lose body fat you clearly build independence, self-assuredness, confidence, and other lose-body-fat skills that surprisingly emanate from your mental intellectual potential rather than merely your present physical ability.

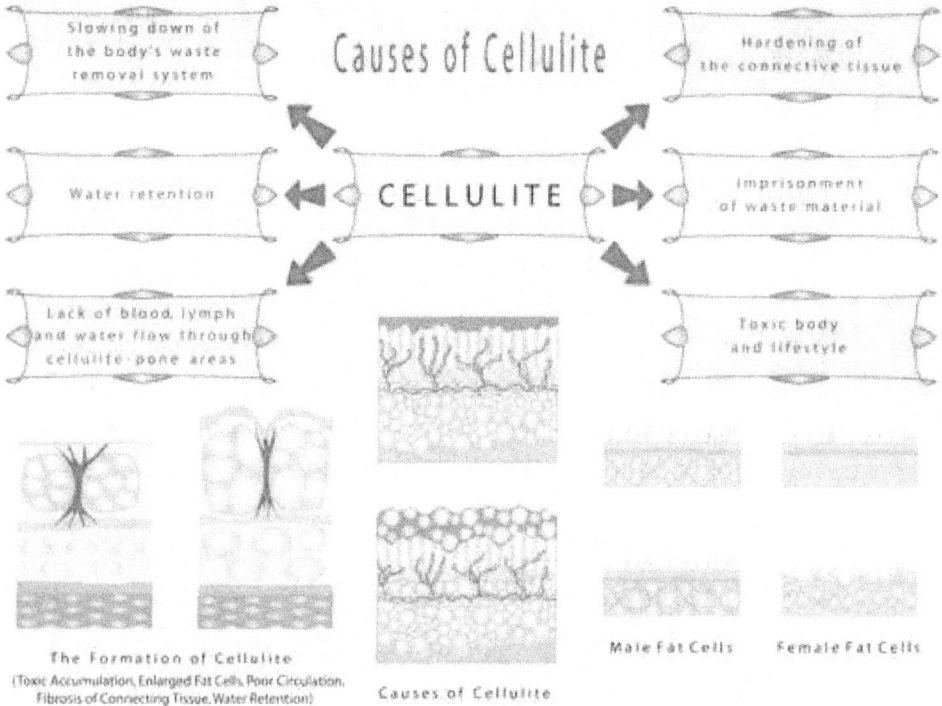

The Formation of Cellulite
(Toxic Accumulation, Enlarged Fat Cells, Poor Circulation, Fibrosis of Connecting Tissue, Water Retention)

Causes of Cellulite

Male Fat Cells   Female Fat Cells

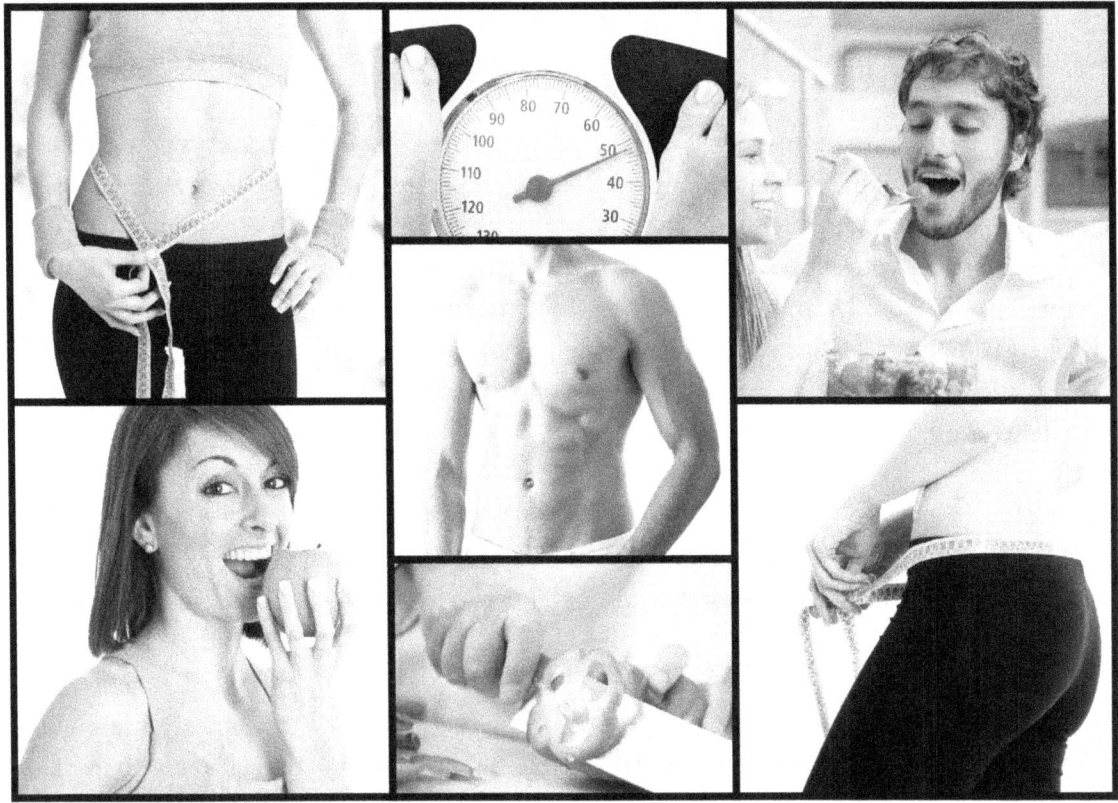

HOW TO LOSE BODY FAT - HERE IS YOUR 3-STEP CURE

Simply do these three things to lose body fat:

ONE: Once and for all, learn how to find out your daily caloric consumption AND your energy expenditure numbers. Both of these numbers are absolutely crucial because they tell you exactly what your body is doing, right down to the very calorie. Once this calculation process becomes second nature to you, full control of the amount of body fat you carry lay right in the palms of your very hands.

In other words, you can shape your "lose-body-fat" fortune and alter your lean body appearance almost exactly how you want it to be.

TWO: Work out for the most part, using much more drive and intensity than you ever have before in your entire life! I say this to you primarily because of 1) remotely conscious human tendencies that we all have toward relaxation and taking the easy way out of a challenging situation rather than facing and conquering its root cause, plus 2) endorsed exercise science knowledge says that performing at higher thresholds gives you life-extending benefits and burns higher amounts of calories from excess body fat. So, to enormously yet safely lose body fat, begin to train yourself towards high intensity interval exercise.

You may burn twice as many calories as you did before, plus feel better and look better, too.

THREE: Lastly, know that the entire weight-loss-lose-body-fat scenario revolves around one, vital and never-changing concept: Being overweight, thus, needing to lose body fat, remains a direct result of eating too much food and not getting enough exercise. Now, with this last one, allow me to isolate your biggest probable obstacle. The number one problem is that you hear this very same lose-body-fat news so much and so often that your brain instantly goes into SHUT-DOWN or shut-off mode. That is, the tendency to assume the "I've Been There Before, Heard It All Before, Done It All Before, and It Never Works for Me" syndrome kicks in immediately.

The solution? Put on some new "lose body fat" ears today, starting right now. Allow yourself to hear the deeper gist this message carries. Cease to dismiss the seemingly small yet crucial matters that make the difference between your continued frustration and your lose body fat reward.

If you need any kind of help whatsoever, just contact us because 1) we care, and 2) lose-body-fat assistance online is both professional and affordable. So, don't worry yourself about spending lots of money to lose body fat.

Understanding the true meaning of what it takes to lose body fat requires acceptance, open ears, and action. So, learn your personalized details, do the required work, plus know confidently and securely almost all about what it takes to lose body fat.

Burn Fat Safely and successfully

Fat burning is normally a leading goal of herbal weight loss pills. The green tea diet is no diverse in that is not only urges but requires the use of simple exercises to be completed along with the consumption of the dietary supplements. Having a green tea diet is associated with several health benefits. One of the benefits is providing a potential cure for cancer.

Green Tea is an incredible, 100 percent all natural, chemical free way to weight loss as green tea greatly increases your metabolism and in addition to that also heightens your body's natural fat burning processes.

A green tea diet increments metabolism and oxidizes fat, and that too without raising heart rates. There are numerous ways to help people on the way to losing weight and some of the most popular quick fixes are the use of fat burner supplements and pills. Fat burning stimulates the secretion of natural antioxidants in the body to counteract the injurious effects of free-radical oxidation caused by anaerobic stress.

Fat cannot be spot-reduced, that is, you cannot target definite areas on your body (like the accumulation areas) with an exercise or two that works those areas. Because green tea diet has an conquering outcome on insulin, green tea diet therefore aids keep sugar from being stored as fats and instead, send them directly into the muscles for immediate use. You need to unearth the perfect Green Tea dietary supplement which contains a large amount of EGCG which increases your metabolism and also your ability to burn fat through its antioxidant capabilities.

The resolution to take supplements is yours. Aside from burning calories and increasing metabolism, these diet supplements are also highly valued to lower down cholesterol levels in a person. Similarly, the antioxidants found in super green tea diet supplements restrain the production of insulin, the hormone that stores calories into fats. Green tea weight loss supplements are also full of anti-oxidants that cause an increase energy use in the body, thus burning more calories.

Having a green tea diet is associated with several health benefits. One of the remuneration is providing a potential cure for cancer. When you switch over to green tea, you get your caffeine, you're all set, but you will deteriorate your insulin levels and body fat will fall very rapidly.

Carbohydrates And Losing Weight!

In simple terms, carbohydrates are broken down by various enzymes into simple sugars then glucose so they can be absorbed into the blood. Digestive enzymes are like biological scissors - they chop long starch molecules into simpler ones.

According to experts, if we cannot burn all the fat we consume, the remainder is stored as fat tissue. This fat-burning ability is determined by the amount of insulin in our bloodstream. [Note: a major factor in insulin release is the glycemic index (GI) value of the carb-foods or meal consumed.] When insulin levels are low, we burn mainly fat. When they are high, we burn mainly carbs. But a problem arises when insulin levels remain constantly high, as in the case of individuals suffering from insulin insensitivity. In such cases, the constant need to burn carbs reduces our fat-burning ability. Result? More fat is stored as fatty (adipose) tissue.

Generally speaking, the speed of digestion is determined by the chemical nature of the carb itself, and thus how "resistant" it is to the activity of the enzymes. A simple sugar is usually much less resistant than a starch, and is digested or metabilized much faster. Things that slow down digestion include: the presence of acid (from gastric juices or the food itself), and the presence of soluble fiber.

High Insulin Levels May Increase Risk of Obesity

This is why experts are linking high insulin levels, together with a reduced ability to burn fat, with obesity. And as you can see, high insulin levels are typically determined by the type of carbs we eat. High GI foods or meals trigger higher levels of insulin than intermediate or low GI foods. This is why the Glycemic Index is considered to be so important in assessing carb eating habits.

As we have seen, the human body is fuelled by glucose. Therefore all foods must be converted into glucose before they can be used as fuel. Carbohydrates are more easily converted into glucose than protein or fat, and are considered to be the body's "preferred" source of energy, and the brain's essential source of energy.

Simple carbs (excepting fruit sugar) are more easily converted into glucose because their molecular structure breaks down faster in the stomach and small intestine. Therefore these carbs raise glucose levels in the bloodstream quite rapidly (less than 30 minutes). This explains why diabetics, who occasionally suffer from an excessively low blood-glucose level, can quickly restore their balance by eating simple carb-foods, like sweets.

Burn Baby Burn: Getting Rid Of Your Baby Fat (After Pregnancy)

One of the joys of conceiving becomes quite obvious as the months go by, and that's showing off your bulging baby bump, a trend being made ever so popular by Hollywood's hottest expecting leading ladies.

But, unless you're one of the Hollywood hotties, you may not be able to shed that baby bump so quickly after delivery. In fact, if you're over 25 and certainly over 30, losing the baby weight may seem like a losing battle.

Not only has our body packed on the pounds during pregnancy, but along with age, comes a natural tendency to favor fat and gain weight. Once a certain fat level is reached and maintained for an undetermined but specific amount of time, the body accepts this (level) as normal and works at conserving it.

So, as you start to purge those extra pounds, other physiological systems kick and foster Re-gain. Hormones and neurotransmitters that control your activity level, your hunger level and how you metabolize food are also affected in ways that encourage fat to make its way back.

But, experts assert that there is hope, it just may take more time and conscious effort. And, they add, that it should be viewed and treated as a lifestyle change, and not a "temporary" diet plan geared at simply shedding some extra pounds.

Among the key factors to dropping the weight and keeping it off is the amount of exercise you do over the long haul. Experts suggest a few times a week if possible, but even that may not be enough. In fact, the ideal amount would amount to about 30 minutes per day, even if it's done at intervals, which is also a great way to help you not only maintain a healthy weight, but stay healthy as well.

Furthermore, studies show that losing weight and keeping it off may mean up to 60 to 90 minutes of moderate exercise daily (for most), and they again suggest breaking it into intervals. You can also incorporate exercise into daily activities such as walking instead of driving, taking the stairs instead of the elevator, etc. And, they caution those who are or may be out of shape to start off slow and take it easy and build up gradually.

Overall they suggest sticking within your (daily) calorie and exercise range and finding a program that's practical and easy for you to commit and stick to. And they suggest making small, achievable goals that will enable you to see results, which will in turn be a motivation for you to continue on your successful path.

FUNNY PHOTOS

WHEN YOU SEE IT
You'll Realize You Have A Dirty Mind

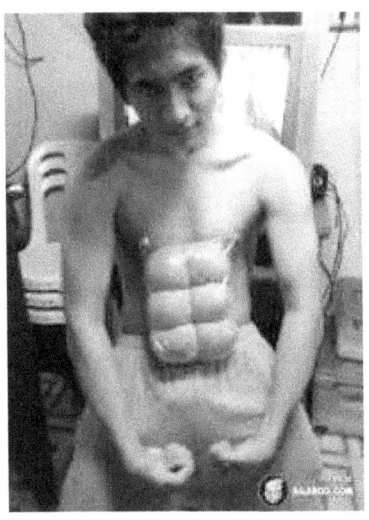

SOMETIMES YOU JUST NEED
TO RELAX AND SAY

FUCK IT!

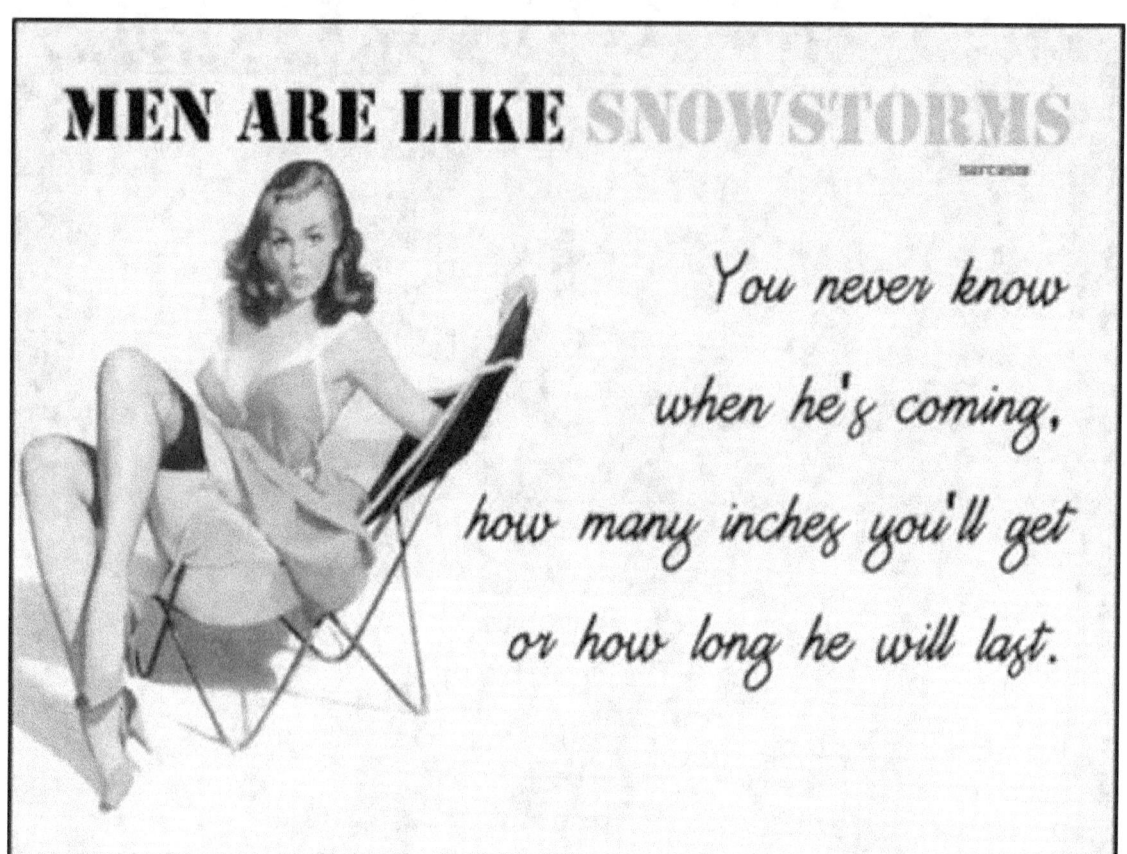

MY FASHION CONNECTIONS
DENIM ALL OUT IN SHORTY SHORTS

"Shorts are an essential summer staple, and for the past few seasons we've seen an up-trending of shorts instead of miniskirts for warm weather," says Shannon Davenport, fashion and media editor atStylesight. "The great thing about shorts is that they can be dressed up or down, so depending on how you style the look, you can get a lot of mileage out of a great pair of shorts."

According to Davenport, there are lots of styles to choose from, including boyish twill, silk and destroyed denim. But if you're looking for something sleek and basic for day or night, there are a few points to keep in mind before investing in a new pair.

"The rise is really important, so if you want to wear a tinier pair, having a higher rise is more flattering, which is also great if you want to nip in the waist or stomach area," says Davenport. "White or colored denim cutoffs are a chic option. Loose shorts are a romantic universally flattering option, and work well if skin tight isn't your thing."

Ready to go short? Read on for some expert tips and tricks on how to rock this look:

KNOW YOUR BODY TYPE

"If you're very short, cropped shorts that go under the knee will only make you look shorter," explains celebrity stylist Anthony Henderson. "Taller people should avoid wearing ultra-short shorts that show too much leg." No matter your height, Henderson says shorts hitting your midway will be the most flattering and are the most workable for day or night.

GET LONGER LEGS IN SECONDS

Wish you had longer legs? Don't fret! Jocelyn Sanchez and Miranda Baham of personal stylist site Stitch Fix say ladies with this dilemma can take a cue from country crooner Taylor Swift. "To add length to shorter legs, throw on a high waisted pair with a shorter seam and add a heel with a bit of height," they say.

EMBRACE YOUR CURVES

Got curves? Flaunt them with the right pair of shorts specifically made to enhance your sexy shape. "For curvier ladies, the cut is crucial," say Sanchez and Baham. "For extra coverage, try slim-fitted dark Bermuda shorts with a longer inseam and a higher rise in the back. Again, you can always add a heel for extra height if you want to elongate your silhouette." If your slim fitted shorts don't include the right cut, you can always take them to a tailor who will create it for you.

GET A TAILOR

Tailors are crucial for making any outfit, including your shorts, fit perfectly. Model and fashion expert Jaimie Hilfiger believes any woman, regardless of her age, can wear shorts, as long as she visits her tailor to get the look down pat. "A major rule is to always make sure your shorts are tailored," she explains. "It doesn't matter what type they are. Having them tailored to fit properly avoids the problem of looking messy or exposing too much."

(Reuters)

GO SHORTER (IF YOU DARE)

"Short shorts certainly aren't for everyone, but there are so many options out there now that no one needs to fear them," says New York City-based stylist Sara Cooper. "Short shorts are a great way to show off your legs, especially if you're long and lean."

Share it with someone you know, invite to our magazine club. Email to My Connections magazine attention eddieadel@weconnect2.com.

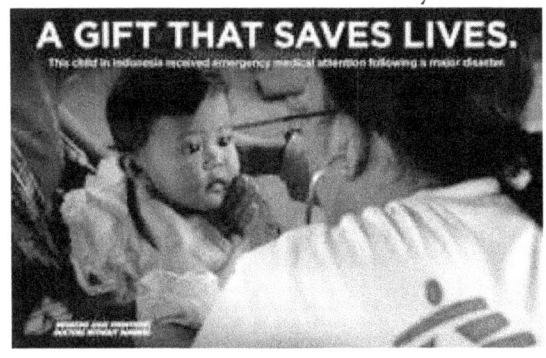

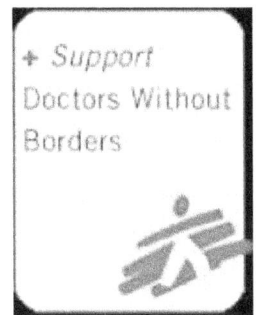

we continue to help almost everyone in desperate need to medical assistance. Thank you for your generous donations. Your tax deductible gift have saved people in 70 countries. Those who are innocents victims of arms conflict, displaced refugees from natural or man made disasters, and in deadly highly contagious epidemics.

We are doctors without borders. we are in the Middle East, Africa, Asia, America, Australia, and China. We deliver medicines and hands on medical assistance to all victims. Visit us at: http://www.doctorswithoutborders.org/

MY FAVORITE PLACES CONNECTIONS

This tie around we are going to put out the worse places and the negative hidden issues and problems associated with it. We are only shortly covering this negative report about these places.

Sea World like you never seen before. The wet and fun place with Shamu is on the negative list of favorite and special connections to the wild and fun time one can really have, as in the past many people share their experience with their love ones and kids as well. What is wrong with this once upon the time highly regarded as a first choice place to visit and spend great fun?. Well cruelty to the big fish have gone too far as the big fish responded in the same manners.

Six Flag was and really will always be a memorable place for myself as a teen. When i went to Six Flag magic Mountains it was all out all day rides, up and down with my high school sweetheart.I picked an equal choice. We were two guy and two girls on the way to Universal Studio, all confused with who really is with what girl. So the two dropped on the ground, and i picked one, that was my choice, but the other girl also had her choice to be with me, but , on the way to have fun, we all agreed on the girl of choice we each picked up from the ground. The excessive police involvement in teenage, gang, and violence inside the park have also spread to the neighborhood around the park to make it a second choice for fun and place to be with family and friends. Let us go also keep in our

on further than the problems places, but mind to be careful and think ahead about destination for our favorite place.

That remind you of that last touch of your meal to always look forward to get to it. Carolina's Pizza and Italian Food in Garden Grove, on the corner of West St and Chapman Ave is the talk of the town, about service. We Serve you food that you eat with your eyes. What you see is what you get. Come on in and indulge yourself.

Take out is our best and final meals. We make sure you have the Carolina's hot fresh and simple delicious flavors experience at home or at work, and if you are visiting our local resorts in Anaheim or in Garden Grove.

Address: 12045 Chapman Ave, Garden Grove, CA 92840

Phone:(714) 971-5551

Open today · 11:00 am – 10:00 pm

Menu: carolinasitalianrestaurant.com

connection or if we were to refer someone to that of a good and fun experience we had in the past before all the problems came about to the Magic Mountains or the Sea World for example.

BEST PLACES TO VIST THIS SUMMER

1- San Juan Islands, Washington

Photograph by Phil Schermeister, National Geographic

Summer in Washington's San Juan Islands is all about the weather, whales, and water. The Olympic Peninsula's rain shadow effect (basically, the mountains block rain-producing weather systems) produces dry, clear, comfortable days on the archipelago's four named islands—San Juan, Orcas, Lopez, and Shaw. Hike in Lime Kiln Point State Park on the west side of San Juan for shore-based orca whale watching or join a Sea Quest kayak tour for a porpoise-level view. Ferry hop to Lopez for leisurely biking, then spend the night on Orcas at Turtleback Farm Inn, a bucolic working farm bordering the 1,576-acre Turtleback Mountain Preserve. The islands are accessible via direct 30-to-45-minute flight from Seattle, or choose the drive-on Washington State Ferry to travel along the San Juan Islands Scenic Byway. The route follows traditional Coast Salish tribal canoe channels via marine highway from Anacortes to San Juan, then continues as two separate driving tours on San Juan and Orcas. Ferries are packed in summer, so arrive early and stay patient, especially on the eastbound ride back to reality.

Pictured here: Sunset warms the San Juan Islands, connected with the Washington State mainland by ferries.

2. Roatan, Honduras

Located about 30 miles north of the Honduran mainland, this divers' dream destination is encircled by a living coral reef, extending directly from the shore. The shallow-water, reef eco-system is teeming with tropical marine life, making the underwater pageantry easily accessible to snorkelers and novice divers. No longer a best-kept Caribbean secret, the largest of Honduras' Bay Islands is working—through the grassroots Roatan Marine Park—to promote sustainable growth by fostering a sense of environmental responsibility among locals and visitors. At the Roatan Institute for Marine Sciences, located on the grounds of the all-inclusive Anthony's Key Resort, guests can participate in government-sanctioned recreational and educational dolphin programs. Options include snorkeling with more than a dozen bottlenose dolphins; unstructured, small-group dolphin dives 60 feet below the surface; and a six-day Dolphin Scuba Camp for kids ages 5-14. For the ultimate Roatan retreat, book an over-the-water, thatched-roof cabana at the secluded Mango Creek Lodge in Port Royal harbor on the island's less-traveled East End. Spend the morning fishing on the saltwater flats or kayaking through the mangrove canals, then float back to your cabana's private deck for some afternoon hammock time.

Pictured here: A diver swims with Caribbean reef sharks in the waters off Roatan Island.

3- Glacier Bay National Park, Alaska

Glacier Bay National Park and Preserve is pure Alaska on the rocks. Glaciers cover 27 percent of this 3.2-million-acre marine wilderness, World Heritage site, and UNESCO Biosphere Preserve, home to humpback whales, harbor porpoises, moose, black and brown bears, mountain goats, and mountain peaks topping 15,000 feet. Mid-May to September, cruise past deep fjords, coastal forests, and the main attractions—seven active tidewater glaciers calving glaciers into the bay. Though most visitors see the park topside from cruise ships, locally owned park concessionaire Glacier Bay Sea Kayaks offers guided and unguided daylong kayak adventures, as well as multi-day rentals for experienced backcountry campers who want to explore the 700-plus miles of shoreline. Additional overnight options include Glacier Bay Lodge (the only lodging in the park) and the adjacent walk-in campground in Bartlett Cove, plus rustic inns, lodges, and cabins ten miles away in Gustavus, Glacier's tiny gateway town. Located about 65 miles northwest of Juneau, Glacier Bay National Park is accessible only by cruise ship, tour boat, or seaplane, or, new for 2011, via the Monday and Wednesday (May-September) Alaska Marine Highway System ferry to Gustavus.

Pictured here: Icebergs calved from Reid Glacier dwarf a visitor to Alaska's Glacier Bay National Park.

4. Roatan, Honduras

Photograph by Ivan Pisarenko, Archivolatino/Redux

Located about 30 miles north of the Honduran mainland, this divers' dream destination is encircled by a living coral reef, extending directly from the shore. The shallow-water, reef eco-system is teeming with tropical marine life, making the underwater pageantry easily accessible to snorkelers and novice divers. No longer a best-kept Caribbean secret, the largest of Honduras' Bay Islands is working—through the grassroots Roatan Marine Park—to promote sustainable growth by fostering a sense of environmental responsibility among locals and visitors. At the Roatan Institute for Marine Sciences, located on the grounds of the all-inclusive Anthony's Key Resort, guests can participate in government-sanctioned recreational and educational dolphin programs. Options include snorkeling with more than a dozen bottlenose dolphins; unstructured, small-group dolphin dives 60 feet below the surface; and a six-day Dolphin Scuba Camp for kids ages 5-14. For the ultimate Roatan retreat, book an over-the-water, thatched-roof cabana at the secluded Mango Creek Lodge in Port Royal harbor on the island's less-traveled East End. Spend the morning fishing on the saltwater flats or kayaking through the mangrove canals, then float back to your cabana's private deck for some afternoon hammock time.

Pictured here: A diver swims with Caribbean reef sharks in the waters off Roatan Island.

THE GIFT OF LIFE IS TO HELP BY ALL MEANS. TELL SOMEONE ABOUT US

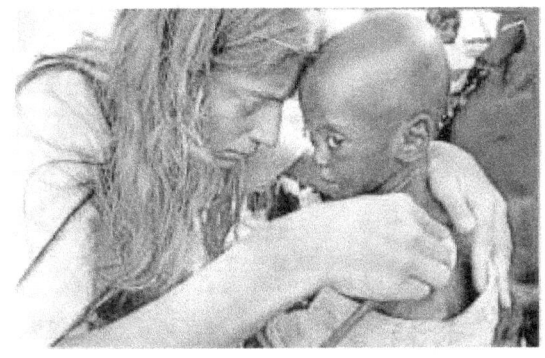

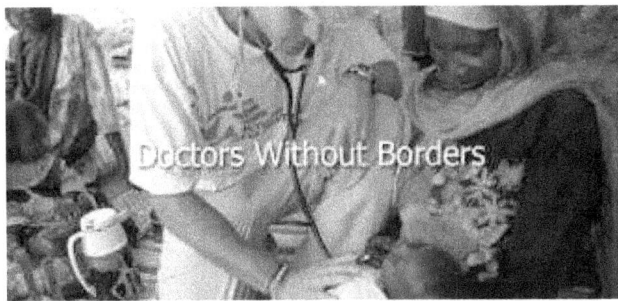

" I FIND DOCTORS WITHOUT BORDERS AN ORGANIZATION OF UNLIMITED BENEFITS TO ALL OF US" EXTEND YOURSELF BY TELLING ABOUT DOCTORS WITHOUT BORDERS TO YOUR FRIENDS, FAMILY, AND TO EVERYONE IN YOUR COMMUNITY. NOW THEY NEED MORE DOCTORS VOLUNTEERS. CONTACT: doctorswithoutborders.org make a donation or refer volunteers.

SUMMER 14 BEST PHOTOS

St. Jude was founded by entertainer Danny Thomas in 1962, with help from Dr. Lemuel

Diggs and close friend, Miami, Florida automobile dealer Anthony Abraham, on the premise that "no child should die in the dawn of life". This idea resulted from a promise that Danny Thomas, a Maronite, had made to a saint years before the hospital was founded. Thomas was a funny comedian, who was struggling to get a break in his career and living paycheck to paycheck. When his first child was about to be born, he attended Mass in Detroit and put his last $7 in the offering bin. He prayed to St Jude Thaddeus for a means to provide for his family, and about a week later, he obtained a gig that paid 10 times what he had put in the offering bin. After that time, Thomas believed in the power of prayer. He promised St. Jude Thaddeus that if he made him successful, he would one day build him a shrine.

In 1957, Thomas founded the American Lebanese Syrian Associated Charities(ALSAC), which helped him realize his dream. ALSAC is also the fundraising organization of St. Jude. Since St. Jude opened its doors in 1962,

St. Jude Children's Research Hospital	TN 38105-3678 (901) 595-3300 www.stjue.org		Thank God for St. Judes and there lovely staff.	
	Thank God for St. Judes and there lovely staff.	Thank God for St. Judes and there lovely staff.	Leave a legacy	Thank God for St. Judes and there lovely staff.
Main entrance	St. Jude Gifts of Donation 	Shown in Tennessee	CRYSTAL GULLERY. Thank God for St. Judes and there lovely staff.	Donation of Books for Parents and Patients $30
Share of chemotherapy for a leukemia patient $75 	GIFTS OF DONATION From kindergarten graduation to prom, so many moments in a child's life are unforgettable.	Help the patients of St. Jude celebrate life. Your purchase from the St. Jude Gift Shop helps in the fight against childhood cancer and other deadly diseases.		262 Danny Thomas Place, MEMPHIS , Tennessee, United States

Taste the freshness of Mexican food at the heart of Orange County Tourist Resorts. located in Anaheim Resort, on Oranegwood Ave, one block west of Harbor Blvd and about 2 blocks North of Chapman Ave in Garden Grove Tourist Resorts. We are local favorite and the Resorts Mexican Food Attraction. Come on in, make your order online or by phone, and we also deliver. See details on our website at: www.micasaanaheim.com

Address: 630 W. Orangewood Ave. Anaheim, CA 92802 | Phone: <u>714-971-0111</u> | Everyday: 11-10pm. Fri/Sat: 11-11pm.

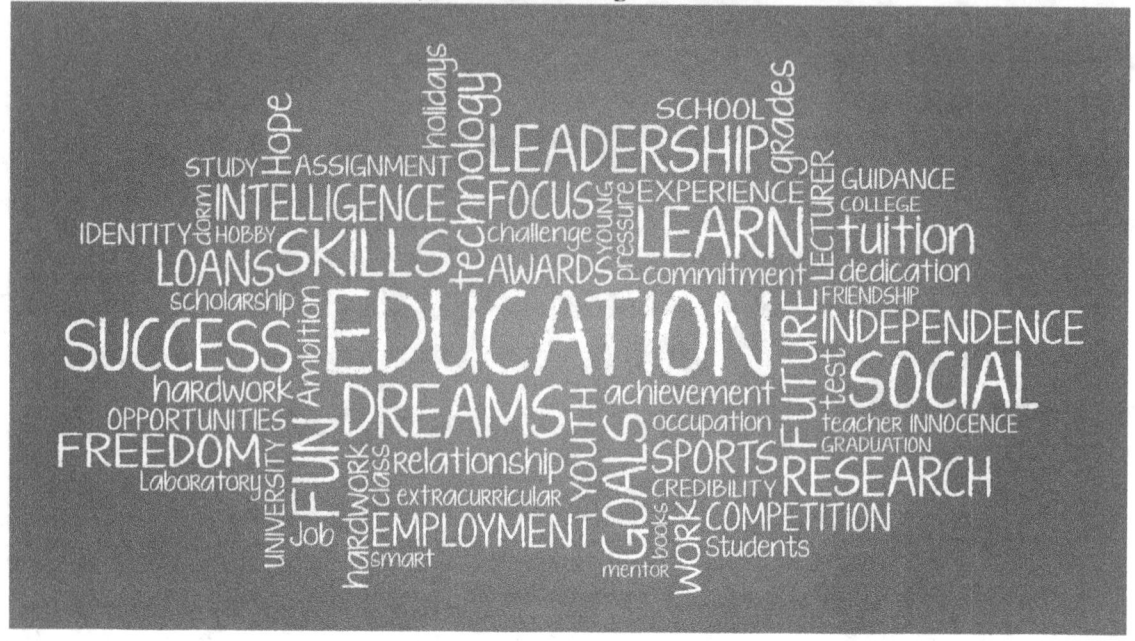

SUMMER PREP FOR EDUCATION
EDUCATION LEAD TO FREEDOM

Education Leads To Freedom

There are many things in life that I care about, but there few things that I get passionate about enough to write about to people I don't know. One of the things that I just cannot talk enough about is education. I believe that everyone who lives in the West needs to understand the absolute privilege and value of education.

I became passionate about education when I lived next to a family growing up whose children didn't attend school. I have no idea the reasons why or even the legal ramifications of the situation, I just know that they did not go and that they never learned how to read or write. I remember feeling really sad about this even as a little girl. Sad because I didn't understand why I got to attend school and learn all these things when they couldn't. And sad because I knew somehow that their lives would be very different than mine because they didn't have the opportunity for an education.

I have continued to be passionate about education because I have a deep belief that education is the primary thing that leads to freedom in the lives of people, families and even nations. If you think about it, many of the choices you make each day would not be in your life if you hadn't had the education that has given you the abilities you have. For example, take reading alone.

What would your life look like if you were unable to read? Pretty different, huh? It is the education you've had that has taught you to read and hence opened up an entire arena of possibility for your life.

What does this mean for you? Well, if you're reading this article than the chances are that you've had the privilege of an education and that you are able to work. It also means that you need to take that privilege seriously and use it wisely. Think about ways of continuing to learn. If you aren't a reader, then that is my first suggestion: become one. Become a person who enjoys the privilege of education by reading and learning all you can.

Another great way that you can use your education to impact other people is to teach them. See what programs exist at local schools and get involved with helping children in their earliest years of education. See what kind of impact you can make on lives simply because you have had the gift of an education. Education is far too costly a gift to be taken lightly or wasted.

Difference Between Classroom Education And Long Distance Learning

What is the difference between a class room course or a similar course by studying and taking long distance examination online? Are online degree, diploma or certification courses recognized?

Well, both have got its merits as well as its warts.

Characteristics of classroom courses are:-

When attending classroom educational courses and programs, you will have the peace of mind that you are actually attending a traditional teaching course although it is just psychological.

You are able to interact and ask questions with your course instructors and teachers.

You will have classmates to discuss issues pertaining to your lessons.

The downsides of classroom educational courses are:-

Classroom courses are much more expensive than online courses because to conduct the courses, the institution you are attending have much higher over costs such as offering its facilities and staff maintaining them.

There is also traveling time to be taken into consideration which is unproductive time loss.

Characteristics of online educational courses are:-

You have the comfort of studying and taking exams from home. Certainly very beneficial for busy people like you.

You save money because online educational courses are much less expensive. This in turn can give you an opportunity to take up a course which you may not be able to afford if the course is offered only on attending classroom lessons.

You will be able to enroll for courses not available near where you live. That is online educational courses are also know as long distance learning.

You have the liberty to decide when to take online examinations since exams can be taken as and when you are ready. However, there is a risk that you may not take the exam because there is no pressure to do so.

You save traveling time from having to travel to classrooms for lessons.

The downsides of taking online courses are:-

The perception that online courses are inferior although many top educational institutions are offering top quality online courses.

Those online education examinations are of a lower quality. Again this may be another misconception because many quality institutions offering both online and classroom education programs set the same examination questions for both their classroom and online students. Even the markers of the examinations are the academics.

My opinion is that enrolling for online educational courses is much more sensible. Many people doubt the effectiveness of the online courses because of the mindset that traditional courses are better. This mindset was created when we were young and attending schools was the way we were brought up. Today, many educational lessons are now conducted online because of advance technologies which were then unavailable.

Critics cited that online courses had no teachers to guide the students. Now, let me ask the critics a question. Since all instructions are on the course materials, why should there be a need for someone to guide you and you pay good money for that? The course study materials are for you to study and most of the time you can email your educators should you have any questions. Therefore, the critic's argument is only for psychological peace of mind.

However, you must be prudent in choosing your long distance learning online educators. This is because since many people have the perception that long distance online education is inferior, then choosing reputable educators and institutions will help to dispel such discrimination.

Accredited Online Universities, The New Path Of Education

More and more colleges and universities are recognizing the demand for alternatives to traditional education. With today's busy lifestyles, many people find it difficult to find time to go back to school without sacrificing existing obligations. This problem is being solved, though, with an increasing amount of accredited online universities that allow for alternate means of earning a degree.

Accredited online universities utilize advancing technology to expose the student to course work required for the degree. This includes televised classes, online chat, emailed assignments and online classrooms. Students will predominantly use the Internet to learn their studies and submit assignments. Some course work will require group assignments that can be facilitated through email or via instant messaging systems and chat rooms. Students can have the same classroom exposure without having to leave the comfort of their home or office.

Before undertaking a program, make sure that it is available through accredited online universities. Do not fall victim to scams offering degrees in a short period of time, usually for a lot of money. Not only are these offers a scam, they can also be illegal. Applying for a job by utilizing fake credentials can lead to many legal issues. If an employer discovers you have obtained a job through false methods, you will likely be fired and may risk both criminal and civil liability. There are currently over three hundred unaccredited universities acting on the Internet to try to defraud you.

Only accredited online universities offer the course load and actual knowledge to help you attain a legitimate degree. Remember that while online courses are designed to take into account work experience and be convenient to attend, they still require effort and time. The idea behind online education is to allow people who are unable to take the time to go to class the flexibility of working during times they are free. However, you can not attain knowledge without research and completing the assignments. A degree that was not earned will not hold the significance of a degree that was earned with hard work and effort.

The Internet is a valuable tool to help in searching for accredited online universities. Not only will you be able to get a list of universities, you will be able to research each one and get a feel for the work required, tuition and educational philosophy. Getting a history of the school will help you determine if it is the best place for your needs. Take the time to get feedback from existing students and faculty before making a final decision. Search the specific university you are considering for possible scams and fraud. If possible, choose a university that is in close proximity to you that you can visit the campus. Since many traditional schools are also offering online course study, this may be easier to do than you may think.

Getting a degree will help expand your career opportunities, enhancing your lifestyle in the process. Be careful to choose only accredited online universities and do not fall victim to the scams running rampant on the Internet. Obtaining a degree takes some time and effort but using online degree programs will add the convenience of being able to set your own schedule and pace.

Difference between Online Education VS. Traditional Education

These days, the internet has grown into a veritable wealth of information for college seekers. Everything from applying for financial aid to taking a course can be accomplished online. Now, a student can even obtain online degrees from one of many schools offering online education as a viable alternative to a traditional classroom education. How different are these two methods of teaching, and do either prove better for the student? There's an abundance of information regarding online education, and distance education is becoming increasingly popular for students everywhere.

First and foremost, there are some obvious benefits in obtaining online instant degrees. For example, juggling a job, school and a home can be very difficult as far as commuting to the classroom every day. With online education, you eliminate the need to attend classes, and instead access your coursework from an internet website. This presents an obvious benefit to the overworked college student because his commute is basically slashed in half. What's more, many distance education programs allow students to complete the coursework any time during the day, while still adhering to overall deadlines. This allows for flexibility that a traditional classroom setting can ordinarily not provide.

However, is an online education truly comparable to the type of education a student would receive in an actual classroom? Many professionals in the field say yes, and certainly students seeking online degrees can confirm this response. Not only does online learning provide a stimulating environment for students, but it promotes even interaction among every student because everyone has a say in classroom discussions. What's more, online education programs allow each student to learn with the methods that work best for them. Plus, many employers respect online degrees as much as a traditional college degree, so there's really no difference in the amount of education or respect a student will receive when attending an online college.

While traditional colleges will never be eliminated, there's definitely been an increase in the amount of students attending online colleges in recent years. Many people choose to follow the online education route for the diversity of material they can find, or because the teachers are more approachable via the internet than they would be in a classroom setting. Students definitely need discipline and self-motivation to succeed in obtaining online degrees, but there's still the same level of help and support from teachers and students online that there would be in a classroom. What's more, internet college students are learning skills that will be beneficial to them in the workforce and beyond because of the way technology is evolving today.

Online degrees are becoming an increasingly popular way to obtain a college education and many students are turning to online education because of the quality of material, convenience and the level of flexibility inherent in distance education programs. Because there's no distinct differences between an online education and a traditional education, students are assured they are receiving the same kind of education that they would in a brick and mortar setting. There are definite benefits to online degree programs, and students with discipline and motivation can and will succeed greatly in online education programs.

Distance Education: Easier Than Ever!

So in order to get anywhere in this life you need education right? And I am not talking about just straight book learning or what you would think about when you think school but everything whether it be a masters in biochemistry or a class in window tinting. The great thing about this age of computers and the internet is that education has become so much more accessible—distance education can be a reality no matter where you are on God's green earth.

Distance education means any type of learning that is taught by someone or something that is some distance away from the learner. The distance could be across town or it could be across the country or across the world for that matter. More and more the universities of the world are offering classes and you can imagine the increased accessibility that people have now to a quality eduction.

So what are the pros and what are the cons of a distance education. First the pros. Number one they are more convenient in terms of being able to access them without moving or commuting. They are also done on your time schedule which makes doing theme while having a job much, much easier. They are also less time expensive as well as less costly in monetary terms. This is because you don't have to deal with the inefficiencies of the human factor. It is often a collection of polished presentations that have been screened for errors and that have been validated before they are offered as an online course. You don't have to deal with the distractions that other people in the class can be during a lecture... and the list goes on.

What about the cons of distance education? Well for one you are not as accountable to others for your learning. You can totally slack off and not be questioned or lose points. Doing it at home can be more or less distracting than a typical classroom depending on the environment in the home. You also don't have a person that is live and ready to answer your questions right when you have them like a teacher in a classroom would be. This is more valuable than you might think as studies have shown that live teaching is on average better than its virtual counter part.

So is distance education for you? It depends on your accesiblity in terms of geography and schedule and also on your ability to discipline your self and motivate yourself to learn. If you can do it than there are many advantages so check it out.

Distance Learning Degrees: The Flexible Route To Higher Education

More students around the world are taking advantage of distance learning degrees and degree programs, thanks to the Internet and the willingness of educators to recognize the fact that many people can't attend traditional school campuses due to work or family obligations. While such issues used to keep hundreds, if not thousands, out of college, such restrictions of time and location no longer remain the key issue when it comes to higher education.

The transition to such opportunities has been a long time in coming, and is long overdue. Hundreds of thousands of dollars of lost earning wages due to lack of college degrees will no longer hold employees back from obtaining the jobs of their dreams, or from pursuing higher goals within organizations. The benefits of attending online schools are obvious, and detractors have little to say. As little as a decade ago, the idea of attending an online school brought snickers or raised eyebrows. People believed that distance learning education programs were just for those wishing to pursue dental or medical assistant careers, though that was, and still isn't, the case.

Major universities around the world now offer online coursework as well as degrees in just about every field of employment, including medical, education, and law enforcement careers, just to name a few. A well-rounded and accredited online college offers students the same quality and coursework as a traditional brick and mortar college, without having to attend classes on campus. In rural areas, or for people obligated to full time jobs and family responsibilities, online college coursework is a blessing.

Such schools are held to the same high standards as a traditional campus, and must pass an accreditation program just as thorough, if not more so, than those given to campuses around the country and the world. Accreditation experts look at student services, coursework materials, testing methods and financial records to ascertain whether or not any school is able to offer expert and qualified instructors and coursework materials. For those seeking information on online distance learning colleges and coursework opportunities, an Internet search will bring up hundreds of online campuses. When narrowing down your list of possibilities, keep important things at the top of your list. First, are student services available, and are you going to be able to talk to a live person during normal business hours? Will instructors be available online or via email to answer specific questions and issues concerning coursework, testing and lecture schedules?

Of course, financing is also important, and while one may expect to pay a little more to attend an online degree program, the extra cost more than makes up for lost wages or the inconvenience of driving to a physical school campus to complete coursework. Many online degree programs offer student financing, as well as student loans, so always check ahead of time to make sure you get the most from your chosen school.

Online distance learning degrees and programs are the wave of the future, and competition is fierce and continues to rise. Do your research, take your time, and find the online college that offers exactly what you need.

Finding Cures, and Saving Children

Facts and Figures: one of the best benefits St Jude Children Research Hospital offer to the public is not about only Children. It is about everyone.

Environmental Health and Safety

The Environmental Health and Safety Shared Resource conducts programs to provide a safe and healthy research and clinical environment for investigators, staff, patients, their family members and other visitors that minimizes exposure to biological, chemical, radiological and other hazards.
Services include:

- Risk assessment surveys of research laboratories

- Assistance to investigators on biocontainment issues

- Field testing and certification of biological safety cabinets (BSCs)

- Employee safety training

- Collection and disposal of infectious, chemical and radioactive wastes

- Online availability of material safety data sheets for laboratory chemicals

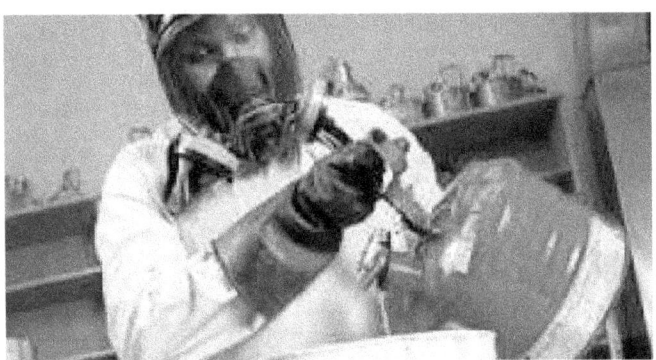

Environmental Health and Safety comprises four divisions:

The Biological Safety division provides a safe work environment that minimizes the risk of biological exposures for researchers, staff and patients. It provides the following services:

- Laboratory surveillance for biosafety

- Assistance in preparation and review of IBC projects

- Assistance in obtaining permits for import of transfer of infectious agents

- Compliance with National Institute of Health (NIH) rDNA Guidelines and other biologically-related regulatory agencies

- Biological safety training

- Biohazard risk assessments

- Select agent registration and guidance

- Shipment of dangerous goods

The General Safety division strives to provide a safe environment for all St. Jude employees, patients and visitors by developing safety policies/procedures, conducting compliance audits and drills. Its services include:

- Occupational safety

- Fire/life safety

- Disaster/emergency preparedness and response

- JCAHO Environment of Care compliance

The General Safety Officer (GSO) assists departments in achieving/maintaining a safe workplace by providing information, investigating occurrences, conducting training, interpreting codes and granting approvals. The GSO has the duty and the authority to take action whenever conditions exist that could result in injury to individuals or damage to property.

The Industrial Hygiene division is responsible for the following services:
- Air quality studies

- Chemical safety

- Containment equipment (fume hoods and BSCs)

- Dangerous goods shipping

- Pest control

- Respiratory protection

- Waste services

The Radiation Safety division maintains a research license, human use license, and radiation equipment registrations with the Tennessee Division of Radiological Health. These licenses and registrations permit the use of radioactive materials and radiation-producing equipment for research and clinical purposes.
In managing these programs, the Radiation Safety staff must:
- Comply with State and Federal regulations

- Provide assurance to institutional personnel, patients and the public that radiation sources are managed responsibly

- Provide services to laboratories and clinics using radiation sources

To accomplish these goals, duties performed by the Radiation Safety staff include:
- Approval of procedures, facilities, and protective devices for radiation sources

- Routine personnel monitoring and environmental surveillance

- Documentation of the receipt and use of radiation sources

- Collection, processing and disposal of radioactive waste

- Evaluation and/or calibration of radiation producing units and survey equipment

- A 24-hour emergency response team

- A comprehensive training and continuing education program

- Periodic audits of the Radiation Safety Program for review by regulatory agencies

MY SOCIAL TRENDS CONNECTIONS

So much of the social media is molding our social living, especially downloading music. Apps too are becoming so much part of our lives. Show down or show time many are in line some place to use their apps for buying something. Credit cards apps, memberships apps, and music apps are really shaping our lives on how fast can we spend our money, or and how fast can we protect our budget. Social media have put many people so close together, it seem like the world gone really smaller .

The Top 7 Social Media Marketing Trends Dominating 2014

With Google announcing earlier this year that social signals are *not* part of their ranking algorithm, some business owners are wondering whether an investment in Google+ is as valuable as previously thought. Add to this the recent decision to remove Authorship photos from the search results, and it's not surprising that some marketers are confused about how Google+ is different or better than Facebook or Twitter **TWTR** +0.65%.

With the head of Google+ social efforts Vic Gundotra suddenly leaving the company in April, and reports of Google+ being 'walking dead', the future of the platform is unclear. For now, business owners should continue to focus on using the platform as a way to connect with prospects, but perhaps more importantly as a primary method of establishing Author Rank and authority for their content. For more on this, see my post Is Google+ Really Walking Dead?

Prediction #3: Image-Centric Networks Will See Huge Success

Image-centric social networks like Pinterest, Instagram and Snapchat may not be serious competition for Facebook, but they continue to draw in a loyal user-base, and that may ultimately be the key to their success.

Pinterest, for instance, is experiencing some pretty astounding retention rates: according to recent research by RJ Metrics, while 2014 has seen a drop in male pinning activity, women actually appear to pin *more* the longer they're on the platform. Robert J. Moore of RJ Metrics writes, "*While the average female user posts 42 pins in year 1, by year 4 she is up to 152! If you set out to build a habit-forming product, that is exactly the type of trend you're looking for.*""">

Prediction #5: Foursquare Will Decline Sharply

According to Foursquare CEO Dennis Crowley, it's not time to write off the platform just yet. In fact, he claimsthe company grew revenues by 600% in 2013, and 500% in the first quarter of 2014.

In an effort to re-invigorate the dying platform, Foursquare recently split its app into two: the original Foursquare, and its new app, Swarm. The new app allows users to easily find friends via neighborhood sharing – without the need to check-in (although you can manually check in to locations if you want to). The new and improved Foursqure app, which will be re-launched later this summer, will no longer allow check-ins, but is instead positioning itself as a direct competitor to Yelp – using its huge database of knowledge to provide personalized recommendations for local search.

Prediction #6: Myspace, Love it or Hate it, Will Grow

While Myspace may not be growing at breakneck speed (that's putting it mildly), it's still hanging in there. In fact, in what some say is a last ditch effort to re-engage users, the company recently sent out emails reminding past users that their photos were still on the site. The email contained the subject line, "The good, the rad and the what were you thinking…" along with a couple of teaser photos meant to entice users to log back in.

It remains to be seen whether this strategy is working: A Myspace spokesperson told Mashable, *"Myspace has been reaching out to current and past users to re-engage them through a personalized experience"*.

Hopefully these efforts pay off. While the platform has seen a significant increase in visitors over the past year (source: Statista), its numbers don't even come close to those of Facebook, Twitter or even Google+. Still popular with music lovers, the platform has a lot of work to do if it wants to attract (or re-attract) a wide range of users and remain competitive.

News U.S. Journal online nusjournal.com

FREE CLASSIFIEDS AT NEWS U.S. JOURNAL

AA- America Anywhere Buy/Sell and other services. Free Classifieds.

for sale (720)
- computers
- computer accessories
- home appliances
- cameras, camcorders
- baby items

- ○ jewellery, watches
- ○ cds, dvds, vhs
- ○ musical instruments
- ○ video games, consoles, toys
- ○ books
- ○ hobbies, crafts
- ○ furniture
- ○ tools, equipment
- ○ health, beauty, special needs
- ○ sports, bikes
- ○ phones, PDAs
- ○ MP3 players, ipods
- ○ clothing, accessories
- ○ Tv, accessories
- ○ other
- ○ Computers for sale..all new ads
- ○

APPLE MACBOOK PRO...
Hi, for sale is my Apple Macbook Pro Retina Display...
$ 1000

- ○

Dining room table...
Elegant solid plate glass dining table with 6 x luxury...
$ 200

- ○

BIANCHI VIA NIRONE...
Bianchi via nirone 7, 18 speed, 52cm Alu Frame with...
$ 600

- You will find easy to self help placing your advertising needs in a lot more categories. News U.S. Journal , nusjournal.com online free classifieds.

- ## News U.S. Journal Free Classified Online Why????????/

- A choice for our readers and visitors.
- Common ground for participation in buy and sale.
- Safe for local and our little towns communities.
- free. yes it is free unless you see that if you want to make fast sale to promote for few dollars.
- great place to practice advertising, sales, buying also. Best of luck . the free classified.

-
- CROSSING BORDERS TO MAKE A DIFFERENCE.PREVENTION, PROTECTION, PROSECUTION.. Abogados sin Fronteras. AVOCATS SANS FRONTIERS.

IN MEMORY OF JOURNALIST SEAN DUGGAS.
HOT TOPIC............The Huffington Posr feature story. Associated Press news coverage:

The victim: The body of Sean Dugas (pictured), 30, was found stuffed in a plastic bag, encased in concrete and buried in the Cormier father's backyard.. - See more at: http://nusjournal.com/little-arabia-after-the-facts-who-to-blame-for-the-chaos/#sthash.ZsAk65 lT.dpuf

Sean Dugas' Body Identified: Man Encased In Concrete Identified Was Florida Man.....

William Cormier, right, enters Barrow County Superior Court for a bond hearing in connection to the death of a former newspaper reporter from Florida, Thursday, Oct. 18, 2012, in Winder, Ga. A judge has denied bond for Cormier, one of the twin brothers charged with murder in the death of 30-year-old Sean Dugas. Cormier's twin brother Christopher was not at the bond hearing because he is awaiting the appointment of a lawyer. (AP Photo/David Goldman) | ASSOCIATED PRESS

DECATUR, Ga. -- Authorities on Friday identified the body of a man who was found entombed in concrete in the backyard of a northeast Georgia home.

The man has been identified as Sean Dugas, 30, according to the Georgia Bureau of Investigation medical examiner's office. The body was found Monday encased in a plastic storage container filled with concrete.

Authorities this week charged twin brothers Christopher and William Cormier, 31, with murder in the death of Dugas, a former newspaper reporter in Pensacola, Fla. The Cormier brothers are also charged with concealing death.

"It's a little hard to wrap your head around it," said Kris Wernowsky, who worked at the Pensacola News Journal, where he sat next to Dugas for about three years. "I've worked there for so many years and covered many things in Florida. You never would have thought you would go to a website and click on a story about someone you know. ... It's heartbreaking."

Dugas' dreadlocks and bushy long beard helped him stand out easily in the Pensacola area on the Florida Panhandle, Wernowsky said. Dugas had covered a wide variety of topics, including breaking news and entertainment, the newspaper said on its website.

Dugas worked for the News Journal from 2005 to 2010, rising from a clerk to a police reporter.

"He was a good breaking-news reporter," Wernowsky said. "He was the type of guy who was eager and loved his job. I rarely heard about him complaining about anything."

Winder, Ga., police officer Chris Cooper said this week that medical examiners declared the death a homicide based on the number and location of the man's injuries. The autopsy revealed that the man died of blunt force trauma to the head about a month ago.

Georgia authorities on Monday arrested the twins at a home in Winder that was being rented by their father. Winder is a small city located about 45 miles northeast of Atlanta.

Police said Dugas had been reported missing and was last heard from on Aug. 27, when he made plans to have lunch with a friend the next day.

When the friend went to pick him up for the meal, he wasn't home. After trying unsuccessfully for days to reach Dugas, the friend went back to his house on Sept. 7 to find it empty. Neighbors told her a U-Haul truck had been there Sept. 3 and they saw at least one man removing things.

That man told the neighbors that Dugas had been beaten and was going to live with him, police said.

The female friend continued to try to reach Dugas before calling police on Sept. 13.

Based on information provided by Pensacola, Fla., investigators, Winder police found the body at the Georgia home being rented by the Cormier twins' father, who told police his sons had arrived from Florida about three weeks earlier. They told him they were supposed to take care of their missing friend's dog. However, they supposedly claimed they'd ended up killing the dog and burying it in their father's backyard, police said.

"There is so much that is not known," Wernowsky said. "There are so many empty spaces for a lot of us. I didn't know any of his family, and I feel sorry for their loss. What a horrible way to end your life."

Jury Deliberations Set For William Cormier, Accused Of Murdering Pensacola Journalist

PENSACOLA, Fla. (AP) — Closing statements and the start of jury deliberations are scheduled for Thursday in the trial of man charged in the death of former Pensacola newspaper reporter.

William Cormier III testified in his own murder trial on Wednesday, telling jurors that he did not kill Sean Dugas.

Cormier told jurors that he followed instructions from his twin brother, Christopher Cormier, when he moved items from Dugas' home in 2012 and sold Dugas' belongings. William Cormier III said he thought Dugas was alive and that he believed his twin was in contact with Dugas.

Christopher Cormier has pleaded no contest to charges of helping William Cormier III move Dugas' body, which was stuffed into a plastic bin, covered in concrete and buried in the backyard of the twins' fathers' home in Georgia.

SHOP DIGITAL STORE AT nusjournal.com Free your choice of My Connections Magazine early issues. Coming soon SUMMER 14 ISSUE.

ALLAA IBRAHIM

Ibrahim Law Offices Lowers Its Fee to File Chapter 7 Bankruptcy to $599....Orange County-based Ibrahim Law Offices recently reduced its fee to file Chapter 7 bankruptcy to $599, making it easier and more affordable for consumers to get relief from financial obligations such as credit card debt and medical bills.

With the court fee for filing Chapter 7 bankruptcy (http://aibrahimlaw.com/ch-7-bk/) set at $306, Ibrahim Law's all-inclusive low fee makes the process economical for even cash-strapped consumers. The affordable pricing presents a rare opportunity in an industry where attorneys typically charge $1600 to file Chapter 7 bankruptcy. "Our new fee of $599 is an amazing price when considering that a highly experienced and professional attorney and staff will be handling the case," Attorney Alaa Ibrahim said. "We also offer free consultation and a payment plan to assist our clients."

Ibrahim Law's reduced price to file Chapter 7 bankruptcy is ideal for individuals who would like a fresh financial start through bankruptcy but have not been able to file because of the high costs that many firms charge as well as for those who are too worried to attempt to file by themselves. With Ibrahim Law's professional assistance, consumers can now take the next step toward seeking legal protection against certain creditors. Here's how it works: Potential clients meet with an Ibrahim Law attorney who will discuss their options and determine whether bankruptcy will assist in meeting their long and short term goals. The initial consultation is an essential step, according to Ibrahim. He explained, "It is imperative that anyone considering filing for bankruptcy talk to an attorney before filing, as there are many possible negative consequence if all the options are not discussed."

Ibrahim Law Offices complete all necessary documents and file the case with the court for its clients. An attorney will be available to attend the bankruptcy court hearing and ensure that the process runs smoothly. Since Ibrahim has also worked with creditors, he applies specialized knowledge to guide clients through the bankruptcy proceedings. "Throughout the process, we will make sure that the client is comfortable and knows what is happening," Ibrahim said.

Chapter 7 bankruptcy does not affect secured debts, like mortgages and auto loans—unless the consumer is planning to return the secured item—but it can be effectively used to eliminate unmanageable debts tied to utility bills, credit cards, lawsuits and medical bills. For more information about Ibrahim Law's lower fee to file Chapter 7 bankruptcy, please contact call (877)) 720-5086 or visit www.ibrahimlaw.com

1300 SOUTH ANAHEIM BLVD.
ANAHEIM, CA 92805
PHONE: 714.827.2810

BOB'S MOTOR HOME

   Bob's Motorhome Rentals has been serving the rental needs of Southern California for the past 40 years. Whether you choose to take a motorhome across the United states, on a camping excursion, or a just a few miles down the road to visit friends, motor homing is an economical and enjoyable vacation alternative.
Bob's Motorhome Rentals and RV Repair, is one of Southern California's Top RV Repair Shops. We offer Interior, Exterior, Electrical, Appliance and Body work. All at affordable prices with an emphasis on Detail!
We are here to serve your rental request & your RV repair needs.
Stop by and visit us at our location in Anaheim, California.
Bob's Motor Home Rentals renting motor homes since 1971.
Let us give you a quote today! We look foward to serving you.

CASTLE INN AND SUITES

Enjoy family fun at Castle Inn&

Enjoy family fun at Castle Inn & Suites, an Anaheim hotel located right across the street from*Disneyland*® Resort and minutes from*Downtown Disney*® District*Disneyland*® Resort ! Our family hotel in Anaheim offers spacious accommodations made for families and groups. This Anaheim, CA hotel is also great for business travelers, and offers upgraded Executive Suites that are great for productivity. Afterward, unwind with an evening of Anaheim entertainment or with dinner at one of many local restaurants.

Hotel Indigo Is Now Open Near the Happiest Place on Earth--Disneyland

The Hotel Indigo is thataway!

More great news for Disney lovers--a Hotel Indigo is opening in Anaheim near Disneyland. Indigo's parent company, InterContinental Hotel Group, has converted the Holiday Inn Express at 435 Katella Avenue, near the convention center, into The Hotel Indigo Anaheim, a "retro-style" hotel with 104 rooms, a pool, a fitness center and restaurant, The Chambers Bar & Bistro.

(The rebranding was made possible by New Century Enterprises, LLC who poured about $5 million into the property.)

As with all Hotel Indigos, the surrounding area and its history play an important in the hotel's identity. But how does this work when the surrounding area is ruled by Mickey? Well, Indigo went way back for inspiration. Apparently, the hotel is located near what used to be a wagon trail that connected several ranches responsible for producing nearly half of America's walnuts in the early 1900s. Seriously. So the Hotel Indigo Anahemi now features mosaic murals with blooming walnut trees. (No nutcrackers in the minibars though.)

Additionally, the hotel's restaurant is an homage to the Chambers Ranch which was home to the families who made their living growing walnuts.

Rates at the Hotel Indigo start at just $159 next weekend. However, the website is still showing some old photos of the Holiday Inn Express but the hotel is indeed a Hotel Indigo now.

[Photos: Hotel Indigo]

BEST DISCOUNTED HOTEL

**Last Minute Hotel
Deals**

Find the best rates on last minute hotel deals from HotelsCheap.org. Save big by booking a last minute hotel.

Welcome to HotelsCheap.org

HotelsCheap.org is a discount hotel provider that specializes in finding cheap hotel rates for travelers worldwide. Since inception in 2002, HotelsCheap has served over one million customers, with hotels, motels, vacation rentals, bed-and-breakfasts, and condos. Operating in 75 countries and supplying over 130,000 cheap hotels, HotelsCheap spans the globe offering inventory from popular brand hotels in North America, to boutique hotels in Europe and Asia, to resort casinos in Las Vegas, even five star luxury resorts in the Caribbean and South Pacific.

If you are on a budget, looking for a cheap hotel, you have come to the right place. Budget hotels often sell distressed inventory at a discount. HotelsCheap.org continually monitors Last minute Hotel Deals to find the very best hotel deal available in your city. If traveling on a budget is you, and you can afford to book your room last minute, finding the best hotel deal in your city just got easier.

Cheap hotel prices are what we specialize in. With a price match guarantee on all room prices found ..

Top Hotel Destinations

- **New York**   Good, 3.9 from 19375 guest reviews

  400 Hotels Available New York City invigorates tourists. Finding cheap hotels in New York is made easy with HotelsCheap hotel coupons! Enjoy the New York culture, Broadway, Statue of Liberty, Empire State Building, Rockefeller Center, museums –

  they're all waiting....   From $40.00

- **Las Vegas**   Good, 3.7 from 28618 guest reviews

  196 Hotels Available Las Vegas is known for Cheap Hotel Rates, as Vegas hotels and casinos often discount rooms with hopes that gaming revenues will cover their expenses. One could argue hotels should give away rooms for free, but since they don't we have the next best thing. At HotelsCheap.org we provide a price match guarantee on all hotel

  rooms sold, so book your reservation today! ...   From $23.00

- **Orlando**   Very Good, 4.1 from 10026 guest reviews

  257 Hotels Available Traveling on a budget, looking for an affordable hotel in Orlando or Kissimmee, you have come to the right place. Save money on your lodging needs by booking online, and don't forget to take advantage of our instant 5% coupons! ...

   From $22.00

- **San Francisco**   Good, 3.9 from 4418 guest reviews

  213 Hotels Available Despite its ritzy reputation, there are plenty of cheap hotels in San Francisco. Finding cheap hotels is made easy with HotelsCheap Bargain Hunter, which quickly identifies the cheapest rates by date and star rating. Check it out and don't fret

about finding a hotel deal. ...   From $21.00

- **Los Angeles**   Good, 3.4 from 3223 guest reviews

   134 Hotels Available Los Angeles is home to Hollywood. Gorgeous weather, fantastic shopping, Long Beach, and status as a world-wide business hub also draw people to the

city. $37>00

- **San diego**   Good, 3.6 from 2907 guest reviews

   219 Hotels Available San Diego abuts the Mexican border. Weather is pleasant year-round making this a winter beach destination. Legoland, SeaWorld, and the San

Diego Zoo are highlights... $38.00

Miami   Good, 3.5 from 5026 guest reviews

76 Hotels Available On the southeast coast, sunny Miami is an art deco haven, boutique shopping, a vibrant nightlife, miles of beaches, and world-class dining keep visitors

happy.   From $21.00

Chicago   Good, 3.7 from 4459 guest reviews

168 Hotels Available Known for outdoor public art, shopping along Magnificent Mile, and Sears Tower, Chicago is a popular vacation destination. Check out Lake Michigan and Navy

Pier....   From $38.00

Our cheap hotels have an average rating of 3.8 out of 5 based on 78052 reviews.

Sponsors and advertisements

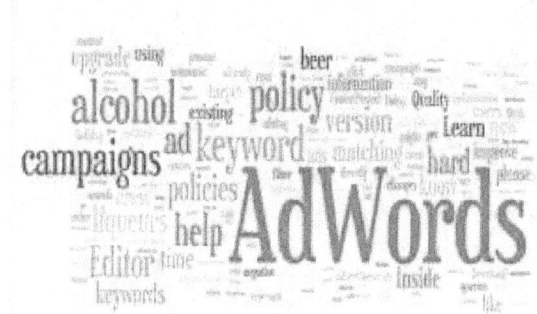

Great advertising programs include a direct google Ads campaign . Your choice of website, your budget, and our beat part artwork make one scream. myconnectionsmagazine.com is one of our digital and publishing websites. Visit us at weconnect2.com, nusjournal.com. newsusjournal.com, policewithoutborders.com, deleonpost.com, anaheimpublishing.co, visioninfurniture.com/blogpost, weconnect2.com/blogpost, policewithoutborders.com/blogpost. and usolclassifieds.

Best Choice free coupons: Simply Clip Ready to go shopping or help someone.

SAVE $1.00

Ziploc®

on any TWO Ziploc® brand bags

SAVE $1.00

LLOYD'S®

on the purchase of any one (1) LLOYD'S® Barbeque Tubs product

SAVE $1.00 ON THREE

Old El Paso™

when you buy THREE Old El Paso™ products (Excludes Old El Paso™ Refrigerated, Frozen OR Soup products)

25¢ OFF

DAWN®

ONE Dawn® Product (excludes trial/travel size)

SAVE $1.00

Kellogg's®

on any TWO Kellogg's® Nutri-Grain® Bars and/or Kellogg's® Special K® Bars

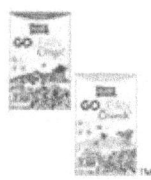

SAVE 70¢

Kashi®

on any ONE Kashi® Cereal (6.5 oz. or Larger, Any Flavor)

SAVE $1.00

Mott's®

on ONE (1) 64oz. or 6-pack 8oz. bottles of Mott's® Fruit Punch Rush, Wild Grape Surge or Strawberry Boom

$4.00 OFF

PANTENE®

TWO Pantene® Shampoo, Conditioner or Styling products (excludes trial/travel size)

SAVE $1.00

Margherita®

on any two (2) packages of Margherita Packaged Products

SAVE $1.00

Campbell's® Healthy Request®

on any THREE (3) Campbell's® Healthy Request® soups

BUY 3, GET 1 FREE

Pringles®

Get ONE Pringles® Full Size Can when you purchase any THREE Pringles® Full Size Cans (Max Value $1.50) (Redeemable at Walmart)

$18 BIG BUNDLE PACKAGE

Picture People

25 Portraits of your favorite pose

SAVE 40¢ ON TWO

Pillsbury®

when you buy any TWO Pillsbury® Crescent Dinner Rolls (excludes Twin Pack)

SAVE $1.00 ON FOUR

Totino's®

when you buy FOUR any flavor/variety Totino's® Crisp Crust Party Pizza® Products (Excluding Party Pizza Pack and Big Party...

SAVE $0.75

Smucker's®

when you purchase any Smucker's® Natural Fruit Spread.

SAVE 40¢ ON TWO

Pillsbury™

when you buy any TWO Pillsbury™ Sweet Rolls, Grands!™ Sweet Rolls or Cinnabon® Bakery Inspired Cinnamon Rolls

SAVE $1.00

Challenge

on any one (1) Challenge Cream Cheese (Redeem at SAFEWAY, VONS/Pavilions, Randalls or Tom Thumb)

SAVE $0.75

JOHNSON'S® Baby

off any JOHNSON'S® Baby product (excludes sizes 1 oz. to 4 oz.)

BUY 1, GET 1 FREE

BEAR NAKED®

Buy ONE BEAR NAKED® Real Nut Energy Bar and get ONE BEAR NAKED® Real Nut Energy Bar (up to a 98¢ value) (Redeemable at Walmart)

More Free Coupons, Simply Clip and ready to Go Shopping.....

SAVE 20% OFF ANY ITEM

Spirit Halloween

Receive 20% off any single item at Spirit Halloween or SpiritHalloween.com.

SAVE $1.00

Emerald®

On One (1) Emerald® Nuts Canister

$3.00 OFF

ZzzQuil™

any (1) purchase of ZzzQuil™ Scented Sleep Enhancer

SAVE $1.00

Ocean Spray® Grapefruit Juice and Juice Drinks

off any one (1) Ocean Spray® 60-64oz Grapefruit Juice Drink

Tide

Detergent, PODS™, Boost, Washing Machine Cleaner and more!

Olay

Look fabulous and save up to $7 on some of your favorite Olay products

PANTENE®

Want hair that's healthy all the way to the end? Put Pantene to the test.

Hungry Jack®

with the purchase of any 1 Hungry Jack® Syrup

SAVE UP TO $47

with P&G Coupons

Get the brands that get you in the game. Save on Braun, Gillette, Old Spice, Charmin, Bounce and more!

SAVE $0.65

Bumble Bee®

on any TWO Bumble Bee® Snack On The Run! Ready To Eat Kits with Crackers, Any Variety (Available at Walmart)

SAVE $1.00

COOL WHIP

when you buy ONE (1) tub of COOL WHIP Topping (any size) and TWO (2) boxes of JELL-O Pudding Mix (any size)

SAVE $1.00

HARVESTLAND®

on any ONE HARVESTLAND® Product

SAVE $1.00

LISTERINE®

on any Adult LISTERINE® mouthwash (Valid on 1.0L or larger)

SAVE $1.00

S'MORES

when you buy any ONE (1) KRAFT JET-PUFFED Marshmallows, ONE (1) HONEY MAID Grahams, AND ONE (1) HERSHEY'S Milk Chocolate

SAVE $1.00

Scrubbing Bubbles

on any Scrubbing Bubbles® Bath Cleaning product

SAVE 50¢

Campbell's® Chunky™ Soup

on any THREE (3) Campbell's® Chunky™ Soups or Chilis

SAVE 50¢ ON TWO

Nature Valley®

when you buy TWO BOXES any Nature Valley® Granola Bars (5 count or larger), Nature Valley® Granola Thins, Nature Valley®...

SAVE $0.75

Barilla®

on TWO (2) Italian-Style Entrées, any variety (Available at Walmart)

SAVE $1.00 ON FOUR

Progresso™

when you buy FOUR Progresso™ products (excludes Progresso™ Pasta Bowl)

SAVE 50¢

Campbell's® Homestyle

on any TWO (2) Campbell's® Homestyle soups

SAVE $1.00

SPAM® products

on the purchase of any one (1) SPAM® Meals for 1 product (10 oz.)

$2.00 OFF

ALWAYS®

ONE Always® Infinity Pad 12 ct or larger AND ONE Always® Pantiliner 30 ct or larger (excludes trial/travel size)

$1.00 OFF

HERBAL ESSENCES® BODY WASH

ONE Herbal Essences® Body Wash (excludes trial/travel size)

SAVE $1.00

Campbell's® Dinner Sauces

on any TWO (2) Campbell's® Skillet, Slow Cooker or NEW Oven Sauces

This is free printable coupon and using discount offer codes where you can find as much as $20.00 of carton cigarettes such as Camel, American Spirit, and Marlboro.

Printable Coupons momysavesbig.com and cigreviews.com

Finally our best wishes for all of you readers and our digital network visitors in the 2014 scool year.

Our detail business information on file at weconnect2.com

To contact us, send all inquiries to weconnect2@live.com

Cigarette Coupons

Home

Virginia Slims Cigarette Coupons

Description

Virginia Slims Coupons are one of the most difficult cigarette brands to find or receive coupons for. You can sign up with Phillip Morris at their main site and select Virginia Slims but I have not heard many success stories with receiving coupons for $4 dollars off a carton like you would normally get with Marlboro. Other good ways to find Virginia Slim Coupons are to search sites like Ebay, Craigslist, and especially coupon forums. Here you will usually find people who have actual printed coupons in hand and are willing to give them away or sell them for a buck or two.

Coupon Information

Virginia Slims 120s Cigarette Coupons

Online Shop Coupons for Virginia Slims Cigarettes

Enter Code:

PAYLESSCIGS

to save up to 10% off your order.

Virginia Slims Coupons Direct from the Manufacturer

Sign up for coupons at - Smokers Welcome Or Call : 1-800-438-0611

Sponsors and Advertisers

GOOGLE AND THE PEOPLE BEHIND THE TOP SEARCH ENGINE ON THE WEB

YAHOO......AT nusjournal@yahoo.com without yahoo how we receive our e-mail

DOCTORS WITHOUT BORDERS FROM 'medicine sans frontiers...the best gift to save

life..donate at doctorswithoutborders.org

The furniture people from Visions In Furniture inc..two locations to serve you just browse our

online store visionsinfurnitureinc.co...we meet or beat any furniture deal.

Godaddy..web hosting and online business services.

Fresh Choice Market, fresh quality with low price...

CSUF AIESEC.....everyone is served..The International Association of Students in Business and Economics...

Carolina's Italian Restaurant......over 1000 beer and wine selection to choose from...

FLAVORS IS SPICE OF LIFE. ART, FASHION, ENTERTAINMENT, MAGAZINE IS FUN AND SOCIAL

MY CONNECTIONS MAGAZINE
Southern California and beyond

On sale at amazon.com ,available at participating book stores